# all of me

NANDINI JOSHI

First Published in January 2022

**ISBN: 978-93-5472-887-7**

**BLUEROSE PUBLISHERS**

www.bluerosepublishers.com

info@bluerosepublishers.com

+91 8882 898 898

**Cover Design:**

Geetika

**Typographic Design:**

Namrata Saini

**Distributed by:** BlueRose, Amazon, Flipkart

for

all those who think writing is just about owning your story,
you are wrong.

- imagination

My dearest reader,

This is the first time I am writing to you as a poem. You may like me or hate me but please, before my end, feel me ONCE with the heart or agony.

ALL OF ME is a collection of modern poetry which speaks on the universal truths of a human being – Life, Love, Hatred & Death.

It makes one believe that life is unpredictable and gleams on the growth one has on the journey of life.

It has poems of love where the lover has only love to offer regardless any finest emotion of one's heart.

It discourses about heartbreak and betrayed feelings of the lover who loved you out of nowhere and out of respect and dignity.

It even comments on eternity and immortality, poems on death can make you realise that it's just death which is your own and none other than it can liberate you and pleasure you more.

I wrote these words in different states of my mind showing good, bad and ugly, I wrote these words to know more about myself but now I think I'll know more about you.

So, here I am, giving a birth to my second one, which took complete NINE months to form it's limbs, bones, ribs and to completely become ALL OF ME.

# Contents

# Life

# What colour is the sky today?

i' ll tell you, how the sun rose,
and moon disappeared,
but can it define,
what colour is the sky today?
i' ll write about clouds,
which constantly moves with me
and stars which silently disappears,
but will they tell us about
what colour is the sky today?
i' ll gather every bit of knowledge
about skies and galaxies
and about how sun reaches to the other side.
i can even tell you how sunrise and sunset belong to the same sky,
but will it tell us
what colour is the sky today?

# Skin

i wear my skin for all day long
but when i try to walk with it,
it decelerates my speed.
i try to sit with a pride of it,
but it's nature distracts me.
i see it
as the reflection by the sun
like a drop of water in the ocean
is known to be the pearl of crown.
it is beautiful,
but it makes me abash
and inside it, i hide all of my me,
as it makes me start with a warm hellos
and tenderness in my goodbyes.

# Seasons

i waited for so long
to watch snow falling
from the heaven of sky
to the hell of soul – heart.
i seek to feel warmness without love
and want to see myself growing
like flowers of spring
without chemicals and pesticides.
i preserved my blushing colours,
to be strong as ice and not to melt into cold water.
i want to dive in the pools of blueish tears
fantasizing myself falling for the unrealistic world of poetry,
all like the leaves of autumn,
i change like seasons,
unlike those who adapt them.

# There are times

there are times,
my soul tremble in fear,
when men stare me with a sinful grins on their faces.
there are times,
i cross fingers out of peril,
when i step outside my doors.
there are times,
my body keeps asking me to stay
for the longing of my pleasures,
but i refuse,  as i am selfish to earn.
there are times,
i refuse to accept the flux in me.
but the only thing i know,
is how a change can change everything.
there are times,
i surrender to brawl on your mouth,
which constantly humiliates me
and violates my body,
there are times,
a glimpse of my structure in the mirror,
frightens me.
there are times,

i offend world with my senses
which isn't an universal taste.
there are times,
i want to gleam like others,
and flaunt every bit of my sense.
there are times,
i beg for time,
from myself to myself.
there are times,
i gasp out of crying,
realising that i am all alone,
fighting a war to just survive peacefully,
unlike to win.

# A Poet

i am a poet.
i make art out of letters,
and when i do,
i surrender my reality
and take a charge on
fantasising.
love or hatred,
life or death,
i imagine
even if it is hell.

*i wish i could smell poems running wild inside my head.*

# What's The Devil Afraid Of?

mother says,
"monsters are devils."
i ask,
"what are men then?"
a creepy silence answered me.
when i see crowd turning towards me
i get afraid
of what if they shut my mouth,
and do not let me scream and cry and call for help?
what if they torture me if i break my silence out of all the noises they put inside my head to stop me?
i don't know why would they pretend to be the truth of this generation?
which they aren't!
but i'll try to probe,
of what's the devil afraid of?
and then maybe i can tell,
that they all belong to hell.

# They Will Say

they say believe,

believe in what you think and do,

why don't they experience the pain in believing which i do?

they say hope,

hope for the best.

what if i am destined with the worst?

they say be kind,

be kind as it's the only language which the deaf can hear and blind can see.

what if i am forced to be cruel?

they say stay positive,

stay positive as it will lead a healthy life.

what if i want to die early?

they say, say and say,

but what if i don't want to hear?

what if i'm tired?

i ask this, because i am tired.

i am so very tired.

my brain is fatigued from believing

my heart is exhausted from hoping

and my pessimism surrounds me with ferity.

## Self Love

beyond the clouds,
i see some love.
not sure if i am standing on the roof or my windows are calling me near.
but something grabbing me with fear.
observation answers,
"the prince charming of your dreams has come, princess! "
the book reads uncountable words after this,
but...
do that princess love really exists?
do love is for real?
do love is enormous?
do love hurts?
do soulmates live?
these precious questions forces my eyes to shut and opens my mind to think.
what is love after all these love stories?
is love really that beautiful how we see it framed in movies and books?
i look up to the sky,
stars are shining peacefully like usually
in a galaxy where constellation is so violent and toxic,

and i imagine a charming, handsome prince on white horse
coming to take his queen away
from the chapters of loneliness and sorrows.
but, i bet,
my imagery thoughts are bigger than my reality senses.
and the prince is no where,
in the whole book of princess's life.
and then i decide,
to precise,
the meaning of love for her rise,
and then the climax arise,
"she is the queen of her land and rules,
no one to judge and accuse. "
and the book reads it twice.

# Will You Ever?

i ask you.
pardon me if i am wrong.
will you ever think aesthetically?
will you ever be able to be silent?
will you ever listen to them just as a song?
will you ever try to receive the worst ones?
will you ever be able to accept that you are selfish?
will you ever be a symbol of poetry?
will you ever be soft instead of strong?
will you ever be kind instead of contended?
will you ever?
i think you'll never.
because
he never made us
we made ourselves.

# Worthy Emotions

we make ourselves strong and contended
but we forget
to demand a breakdown too.
is this for self love?
then isn't this a necessary emotion to feel too?

*my art is like wearing poetry.*

# Society

i am me

because of it.

you are you,

because we have made you.

- society

# Dear daughter,

you will be like me, a strong zest. i know you'll be my baby feet, for once and for all. you'll be slow and subtle, as like i am. you'll walk and teach us how to run. you'll talk and teach us how to sing.

one fine day, you'll grow too, like a plant and will never stop growing. but there will be chances, where you'll be dried up and you'll have no one to garden you and your roots. for that time you should learn how to water yourself.

daughter, you'll bleed too. but i want you to smile when you are bleeding. i want you to feel your scars and wounds. i want you to experience every feeling of your phases in an indeed way because every phase has it's own beauty and i want you to believe that you grow better day by day.

i will never say that you'll be happy all your life, instead i want you to accept that this is life and you can never ever escape from it. sometimes you'll even have to bring new hellos and bid an adieu at the same time in your life. i know this can make you fragile, but i assure you that you'll do it because you are so much stronger and powerful than i am. sometimes you'll have to be a hurricane and an umbrella at the same time to know what's best for your loved ones. you'll get through all of this, no matter what.

you'll be papa's favourite and a pride to look into mirror. you can make him hopeless when you yourself will be hopeless. none other than that thing can make him feel prideless for his daughter and you have to believe it.

"hope is the thing with feathers that perches in the soul. "

we want you to never ever lose hope in yourself. you are precious for us, your mistakes will make you learn, it can create conflicts too, but it can never ever make us unlove you or make you love less. i can't assure you that you'll not be punished for your mistakes, but i can assure you that you'll be loved. no matter what. mark my words.

that is why, i don't want you to hold onto grudges with us, i want you to understand us as parents, that we care for you and we don't want you to break. instead we want you to be still and strong like an old tree.

we love you.

mama and papa

# Smoke and mirrors

every night  
i see myself.  
harmed and destroyed peacefully in the mirror.  
satisfied, it says!  
none like me, questions it anyway.  
every night  
i dwindle.  
smoke it is.  
which makes me wane.  
one's making me lessen,  
and other's making me sane.  
i am fading, like a moon,  
in a starry and smoky night.  
but the moon doesn't have mirrors to answer.  
i seek help from them,  
but all they can do is to condemn.

# Lost

i am lost
while finding myself
in the forest of fame and pain.
my truth holds me but i couldn't find it.
to what to choose and what to drop!
i must know myself
what causes me agony
and what cures my aid.
what's stopping me and what's pleading to take a step?
i can't find my answers.
i am full of words
or
i say,
full of swords.
but i don't know,
how do i put them in a form
or
i say,
how to use it in a war.
where reality is at the endpoint
and imagination at start.

# There Is Always Tomorrow

singing singles,
dancing with a crowd,
living the whole day with some rhythms of tomorrow.
sun comes and moon disappears,
and the cycle is on road.
entity will move,
even after an expired time.
there is always tomorrow
to get up
and move yourself
on the beats of life.

art is also an ART.

# Fame Is A Fickle Food

fame is a fickle food.
fame is junk.
changes every now and then with the trend.
you'll drown in it at once'
and when you'll try to comeback,
it won't let you go.
as if it's a swamp.
it's  like a dreamland.
from which reality is far far away.
it's fickle.
some may negotiate
and some may quash.
it's like feign.
cease you to liberate yourself
and make you a stranger in your own head.
either of the ways,
i can say is that
it's a fickle food.
some can stodge,
and some won't even get hungry.

** you'll be seen,  heard and touched and still feel unnoticed, like a ghost. **

# My faded fantasy

ever since i was small,
i have had a fantasy,
to die in love.
to extinguish that flashing fire in my heart.
passionate about singing chorus of fame and fantasy together.
as i grew up,
i found that fantasies are way too bold for me to accept and attain.
so,  i settled my way to fame,
where i was alone and the world was screaming my name.
i felt the missings,
but i couldn't find what all they were.
like a pretty bloomed flower,
one loves me for my fragrance and one loves me for my body.
but all which was left were my fantasies.
alone in the dark.

# I Am A Poem

i am a poem
i want my name
clearly in seven letter word.
i don't want to be known by others.
i am not gonna die like my mother.
i am gonna be my own words,
whatever it asks for,
poverty or worst of smells,
i'll write,
like the words are left with so less time.
i am gonna use freedom as my poetry.
i am gonna be the free bird
whose cage is set on fire
and wings just to fly and fly.
and when it tumbles, it will learn how to rise like a sun.
so, bury me like a human when i die,
but please,
let me live and breathe like a poem,
which is deep and sensed by all.

# Write And Bleed

i write and write.
poems after poems.
and then i stick them in the drawer,
they sit there in the dark,
without any complaints and demands,
they breathe where no light shines
but still beams whenever i read them.
i bleed and bleed,
words after words,
and then they all dries up like the ink on the paper.
they sit there,
on their own places,
where they yearn to speak emotions,
yet they make me wail.

# I Have Seen

i have seen,

snakes and vampires,

crawling and running inside me and sometimes seated in peace, somewhere in the corner.

and darkness found me in a room full of gleaming lights.

i have seen,

plenty of ghosts, haunting me from a toxic essence of love.

and each demon sitting at my limbs

and operating my ribs to collide with my heart and bones.

i have seen,

dancing bandits in my pool,

asking me to share myself with them

like a slut.

and kids who choke out of poison, who dream when they see a flying plane.

i have seen

killing and raoing truths and visions of feebles and frails.

and kidnapping autonomy from the minds of dear delicate darlings.

i have seen,

dogs drinking whiskey

and smoking in inebriating eyes.

and their theories of risking breath on alias.

i have seen,
myself writing poetry on lovely heartbreaks,
and me, myself and a me i am going to be.
i have already seen,
saying sorry to my kids
and my esteem killed at my own risk.

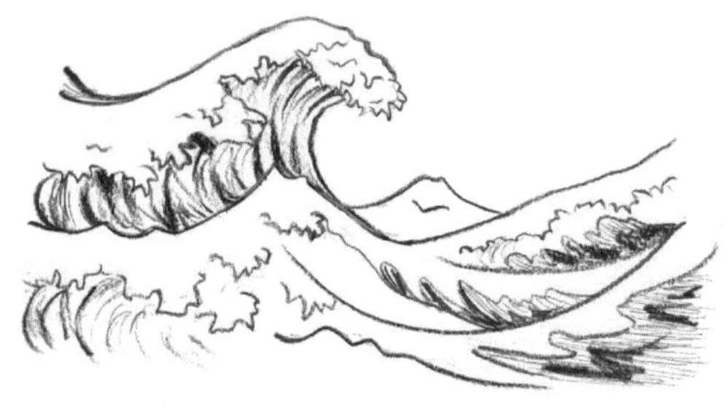

**i'll hear poetry like a deaf man.**

# Love

# You In My Dreams

i saw you in my dreams again
you were so happy
and i was looking at you.
that spark,
that orangish fire in your eyes could burn bridges.
they made me feel alive
and warmth of you in that january air.
i was craving
to be what you want me to.
that starry dark night also felt something about us,
exactly what i feel for you.
i don't mind if it is 10 degrees or -2 degrees
as long as your presence will keep me warm with a hug and a cigarette you blew,
i'll be happy.
i saw you in my dreams again,
and this time it felt more real than every time.

***you are my dream and i don't want to wake up***

# You

the more you see through my eyes
the more you will love yourself.
you.
you are the longest hug my husband has given me ever
you are my whole cake instead of that last piece which was wanted by all.
you are pure as water, clean as air, and important as oxygen.
you.
you are that minor difference between good and best,
you are the sun, shining bright even on your worst days.
you are an excavator, who is always busy finding my historical wounds and love bites.
you are my waves in the ocean.
you are the lucky pen for that famous writer in the town, who is fighting against your fiends and mine.
you are like a shadow,
who meets the body even in darkness.
you.
you are oxygen, carbon, hydrogen, nitrogen, calcium, phosphorus, potassium, sulphur, sodium, chlorine and magnesium,
because the human body is made of them.

when my type of me and you kind of reacts together, the
substance produced at the end of the reaction is different
from others, you know why?

because there's a part of you, and you make those chemicals
turn into subtle colors from their transparency.

you are the moon, which shines calmly into the multiverse,
which changes patterns and shades.

you are the cosmologist, who studies my eyes as stars,
planets as hearts and love as galaxies.

you.

you are a candle which lights my dark eyes,

you are mr bingley to my beloved jane

you are an algebraic equation, and while trying to find x i
found y.

you are my mind with curiosity,

yes you, my love,

you are my last love.

because sometimes, it's the last love that only needs talking.

## Reasons I Fell For You:

1. it's how you see someone smiling and it makes you smile too.

2. maybe, it's how you splash the oceanic adam's ale when you sit beside me to listen to my silence.

3. it's how you want to sit under a naked sky and see a falling star with me.

4. it's those little things which you do to fix me, as if i am broken.

5. it's how you want to paint your own galaxies and constellations inside your mind with me.

6. it's how you put your head on my shoulder and want to travel the whole paradise.

7. it's how you want me dead, because you know how much i love dying.

8. it's that small 4 letter word which has no syllable at all and you make me feel that every night.

9. it's your presence which makes everything like a book, everyday folding a new chapter.

10. and many more, i just cannot write.

# Chasing Only You

i am chasing you

and when i say you,

i mean those eternal smiles and occasional tears.

i'm chasing you

and when i say you,

i mean the skin you fit into and the makeup you wear on terms.

i'm chasing you

and when i say you,

i mean those little things which you do to comfort me and to endeavor being like you.

i'm chasing you

and when i say you,

i mean love.

which defines you.

# Stardust

how?

how can i?

i cannot!

you can.

because you are made up of it,

magical and charismatic.

stardust.

you are stardust.

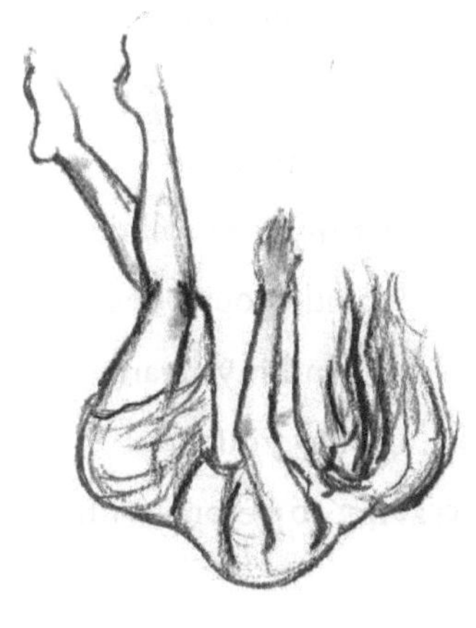

*i don't want to fall in love,   i want to rise.*

*- a random thought*

# Just Let Me

let me flow,
into you.
let my body melt
into yours.
let my ribs collide,
with your bones
and my heart
into your soul.
- craving to be one with you.

# We

we started when we were petals,
and now we are roses.
every thorn is not to be picked out but to care for each other.
our stems have wrapped us to stay together,
roots give powers to fight every storm we face.
we started with planting a seed in each other
and now we are a tree.

*- you & me*

# Lightening

i see a thunderstorm,
a thunderous night in my dream.
from purple to purple,
first blue then black and a sudden purple again
with a white flash sign.
winds making me miss you,
like how passionate lovers are we,
i wish you could make a cup of tea,
and a flavor of love on it with some sweet chocolate cookies.
and that sound of the wind...
my heart beats so fast,
that i cannot control
like flowers from bees
and i want your arms to hold me
and click me in black and white
as like i am a reel of your film,
watching you without a distraction
just you,
for me,
with me
and into me.

# Love Is Love

love is love,

you say.

love is midnight dancing,

i say.

love is love,

you say.

love is driving me back home,

i say.

love is love,

you say.

love is asking "did you had lunch?"

i say.

love is love,

you say.

love is respecting my temper,

i say.

love is love,

you say.

love is "mommy, please don't cry! "

i say.

love is love,

you say.

love is bringing favorite shoes for your daughter,

i say.

love is love,

you say.

love is different perspectives,

i say.

love is not luxury,

you say.

luxury is having love,

i say.

# When I'm In Love

when i'm in love,

i feel excited every second by just glimpsing your display on my screen.

when i'm in love,

i want you to grip me tightly into your warm appendages.

when i'm in love,

i wait every evening for clock hands to move at that particular hour, where we share our drill.

when i'm in love,

i become a poet and i want you to be my words.

when i'm in love,

i sing love me like you do, lo- la- love me like you do, touch me like you do, to- to- touch me like you do.

when i'm in love,

i feel thankful every time for holding me when i was tumbled and downcast.

when i'm in love,

i want you to make me feel wanted, as i do.

when i'm in love,

i read our conversations as if they were my syllabus.

when i'm in love,

i adore you and your pictures like an art.

when i'm in love,

i think and think and think
only about you and you and you.
and when i'm in love,
i love you.

*love me like the world is coming to an end.*

# Eyes

all i know is,
one complex tool,
we call them eyes.
a troubler in all my love files.
not too hard to stare,
and a glimpse of flare.
the signals of my connection is strong enough,
to recognize his site.
he doesn't look at me,
nor he speaks about me.
but you know, these eyes,
always gets me into trouble.
in a blink of an eye,
there are floods and mudslides and destruction all over my brain because of him.
he is my enemy, and my weapon is strong,
so strong to make him fall for me.
my eyes
to make him realize,
my love at first sight,
and one sided too.
to that brownish big shops,
and those small alleys all over the town,

i say thank you.

for making my first love so happening.

the love was in the air

and i was breathing heavily to take all that air inside of me and die,

and with all that air filled with love

i was reminded about my house curtains,

which were floral in the print, and crape in the fabric.

beautifully designed and weaved with emotional embroidery on the borders.

but,

i wasn't satisfied.

i asked the shopkeeper to show me,

the fabric silk and the print love.

he kept pieces and pieces in front of those weapons,

but my eyes were stuck on one.

oh! these eyes, i say!

(recollection of occurred memoirs)

but did you know,

that there are more other complex organs you possess,

other than your eyes, which always confides.

my eyes, your eyes, and some real lies.

after ages and ages, i anticipate,

may this story is brought to you up by your grandchild, for that one sided love,

which my eyes had loved,

and i know which your eyes had discussed,

and which your grandchild is planning to revert.

# Love Isn't Easy

love isn't easy,
isn't easier,
and isn't the easiest of all.
but, you see,
my every bit is about you.
love isn't easy
i say it again and again and again and again.
your camera pixels know me,
better than my parents living all day with me.
this may be the reason why i am so obsessed with your camera.
you must be an umbrella,
for all of them....
rescuing from the unwelcoming droplets.
or maybe you're a cup of coffee
which makes us think hard and make ideas.
sorry.
to those who expect you to be something special like that to me.
sorry.
you are you.
for me and for you.

you are love,

for centuries to come.

and this is a reminder,

that god has not forgotten about me.

for instance,

the bed covers of your bed still smells on love when they are washed, once, twice, thrice or unlimited times with arguments mistakes and misunderstandings,

but,

they still spread the fragrance of the love we had made.

so let's stay in that bed,

for the long years to come.

you love me, like you do,

i love you, like i do,

that's enough and easiest of all

# Love Letters

in my window,
there is some spilled ink
and the mess is all over in my head and room.
all around me is love
that you have poured in my heart,
to digest and to revive my bruises.
my instincts say,
that i should scroll and register
every feel of you holding me and loving me
like an angel.
i'll put it down there in my sheets
that you have loved me without comparing me to heavens
and to good girls.
i'll pen it down that my flaws make you more happy than
my perfectness.
and that love is not all we chase,
but for each other,
we seek faith.

# A Letter To Love,

*december 13th '2010*

i think, to be very honest, i'm feeling loved. in my entire *20* years of experience i have never felt this loved by anyone. though, this makes me somewhat unsure about some things too but it's a way i can think of someone and i can miss being by his side. he has flaws, i would not say he is perfect for me, instead, i like his flaws and how he is so original and natural with me. i can see that creepiness in his eyes and still love him for loving me. the way he sparks his cigarette and the way he puffs, the way he smiles when he is half drunk, i mean, what can just hold me to unlove him? yeah, the fact is that i don't love him for anything, i love him because he loves me, and to me that what matters, the one who loves you is the one who deserves to get that love back for loving you. because anyone cannot just come and love you for who you are like he does. it's not anyone's cup of tea!

i don't know what our future will be, where our paths will end, or tomorrow we will be ending up together or not? i literally don't know. and then this question flies from my mind to tongue, and he asks me "are you happy?" and i reply with a smile on my face, "as of now, for the time being yes! " and after this his one and the usual quoted sentence "that's it, that's what matters. " and it again makes me love him stronger than i did. like this, we have uncountable conversations and the love reaches to infinity. thank you, for loving me like you do, and i hope this will continue, because that is the only thing, which makes me love you.

*- 4:07 am thoughts*

# 2 People Who Stay Together

two people who stay together,
in good and in bad,
in sickness and in health,
in body and in soul,
in best and in worst,
behind and in front,
in fear and in courage,
in fancy and in plain,
in east and in west,
in fall and in spring,
in winter and in summer,
in wild and in tame,
in grin and in frown,
in gain and loss,
in high and low,
in dark and in light,
in death and in life,
i'm beginning and in the end.
(no choices, only ands.)

to die is to live in those lights of life where
i am your wild bee and you'll always be my eave,
warming and nesting me
beneath the parts of the roof.

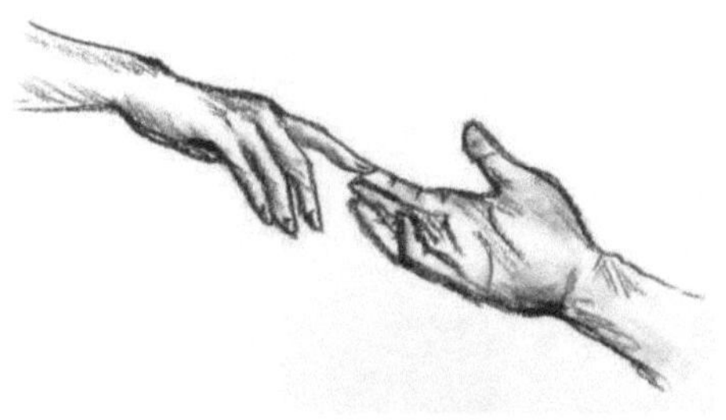

# The Chaos Of Love

when i see,
i am hidden.
when i hear,
i am quiet.
when i touch,
i am felt.
when i talk,
i am words.
when i eat,
i am swallowed.
when i breathe,
i am loved.
- always about him

# I Wish

i wish
i could phrase what i feel.
i wish
i could write what i thought,
and what made me think more about you.
i wish
you could change from words into a poem, who wishes and fulfils
everything i wish for!

# I Like You

*april 4th 2019*

when i see my name on your phone, i hear your voice pronouncing it with a mid note, a perfect pitch and a whisper in my ear. i don't know why, but the only trust i got is in you. i have shared my deepest family facts and my darkest dilemmas with you, without any doubts of insecurity. i don't share it with anyone. i like how you are so practical and atypical unlike others. i like how you make a grammatical correction in my poetry unlike others who be usual in my every draft. i like you, and get some of my best vibes from you. i mean it's been three years and i still can't get over you. i think it' s not my infatuation, but something more to it. i want to keep this simple and plain, like you. no, you are way too difficult to understand but you are way too sober. that is the only spark which flashes again and again into me to explore you from inside out and to know you more. i like how you make me understand things which make me feel love for you. i wish i could just rise with you in the future.

for those who think practical people can't love, practical people are practical in love. they don't often show, or it's kind of a cliche act for them to show off their love in front of people but i know, it's a fact, and i like it. i just like how you are and how you deal with things and how you are a savior for me every time.

thank you, i must say - i like you.

*xoxo*

*yours and only want to be yours*

# Sound Of Love

listen.
stay quiet,  and listen.
it's coming from you.
do you hear that?
if you can't hear then lay your head on my chest,
and listen,
it's peaceful and soft
and sometimes wild too.
it' s the sound of love.
which is all about you.

# Future Lover

dear future lover,

i know,

who you are,

and where you come from.

you are dirty as mud,

and pretty as lotus.

but unfortunately and fortunately,

you come from the same sides.

i want you to be aesthetic and a travel freak.

so that i can write your stories and paste your memories on my house walls.

you will be my future lover,

but you know what makes me sensitive that it won't matter if you will ever love me or not,

but i want you to be my future

because i know,

that i'll make you love me,

no matter what.

only for my fate.

-be my home,
where i can return to.

# Hatred

# Release Me

release me...
i am choking.
please release me.
i can stop by and make you realize,
then why can't you just release me?
i see a judgmental interlocutor
who is good with his words
but doesn't read poetry journals.
i seek and ask for help,
but he declines my urge.
i am an eclectic eclipse
but eclectic is unheard,
and eclipse is only seen,
without paper or a broken glass.
i think that may be the reason,
i'm unheard and unseen.
now i know,
why didn't that interlocutor didn't release me!

# I Am A Liar

*disclaimer: this is a lie, don't fall for it.*

i'm chasing you,
or your demons.
cannot resist to find you
or solace in you.
as it leads to heaven
or maybe hell?
your powers might die but
you are soft and uncold.
singing operas won't help you
to digest this fact.
anyway,
hey see, what truth holds in itself.
you are trapped, like a rat.
one truth in this whole lie,
is that i am a vulture
and i can sense death,
and my death is fascinating.
like you can attack the sick and wounded me
and make me die slowly,
so, you are a vulture too.

but this poem is a lie,
don't get yourself trapped in this
and i am a liar
so please,
don't hate me for this.

** read this poem again with the integrity in your head**

# We

i see,
that you are you,
and i am me.
but we are not we,
and that's how i see.
the last time i saw you,
we were we, not just you and me.
i'm making we,
unlike you are making us.
i'm making us,
unlike you are making we.
i'm making fictional stories about us,
you are making a nonfiction book.
i'm using metaphors,
and you switch into similes.
i am trying to make an ode,
and you unquestioningly put efforts to rhyme our poetry in order to make a sonnet.
just a fourteen line *sonnet*

# Illusion

your love for me is an illusion.
i can probably prove it.
world names this illusion as infatuation.
i am not good with my words, so i call it an illusion.
ever heard the poetries of sea and sky?
they read something like –
"at the end of the day,
sea and sky meets at the horizon,
facing the world
with deep fears and love. "
no!
sea and sky are never meant to be.
they never meet.
this is an illusion,
just like your love for me.
it clears my mind in every way,
and how i used to imagine every illusion like my poetry pleasures.
there is pain,
lingering in my eyes,
to come in the form of tears.
there are words,

lingering in my throat,
to come in the form of a song,
sung by my broken guitar.
there is love,
lingering in my heart,
to come in the form of illusions of my poetry.
there are plenty real things,
which are lingering inside me,
and want to be spilled out,
on an old sheet, but,
stuck like dried ink of an unused pen.
i don't know,
how to present these illusions,
but,
i know, these illusions represent you.

# Thoughts

the words are lingering on my throat,
but i'm sorry,
i cannot speak.
i'm lost,
in a bitter fact of yours.
hiding distinctive feelings for me won't help you.
i better start my conversation with the dark coffee,
to resist and revoke,
as dark as the lunar eclipse.
ok. i am sorry.
i would have tried,
to collaborate my words with your music and my feelings with you,
but, you are just not a drop of water but the whole sea.
so why not just make a poetry?
or a song, that represents just you and me?

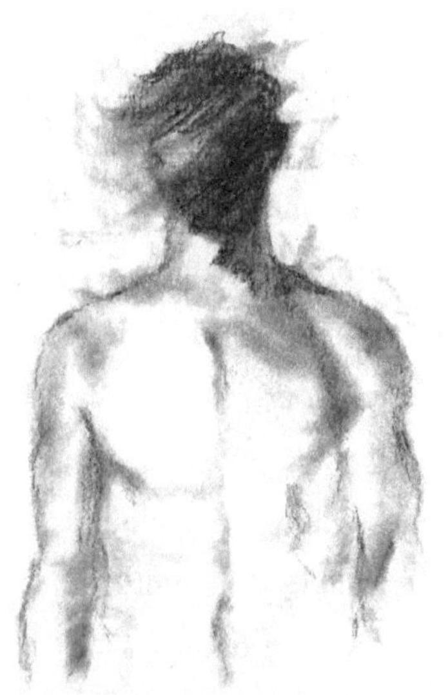

- you are a havoc.

# Tired Me

i am tired of convincing myself
that you are no longer mine.
it's been 29 days and still feels like the first.
how briefly you left me,
mourning and crying.
nothing is healing me,
neither your gifts, old conversations
nor your memories.
it's only you, and your presence
who will heal my wounds.
they said, time will heal,
i want to know,
what if it doesn't?
because i know, it will not.
that particular goodbye was so difficult.
every fucking time,
i remember you saying that word and it makes a part of me dead inside.
do you miss me even half as much as i miss you?
i wish i knew the last times,
i would have kissed you longer, hugged you tighter
and slept next to you for a little while more.

# Comeback

i feel like my heart is broken
into pieces.
which only you can fix.
please
comeback.
i feel like
i am mourning my death.

# A Cheat

your fragrance makes me go wild.
that smell makes me more passionate.
how can i say that you burn bridges?
when you are the fire,
and it's how fire works.
just a spark,
and it can burn a heart.

# Roses

i hate flowers,  i hate roses.
but when you gave me,
it was so cherishable to me,
like a bijou to a lady.
i thought,
it's a witness of your love.
i am sorry i called it love.
it's a witness of you breaking my heart,
as like you are a hammer and i am a mirror.
those broken pieces can never make an orignal me.
you saw me inside out,
my sorrows and my tears.
you heard me up and down,
my laughters and my mourns.
and you knew,
how much i hate flowers.
despite that hatred i accepted them with a monolith on my heart
as evidence of love.
i wish i could tell you,
that you killed me.
and that rose,  it's still a memory kept in my diary

to cry and feel that death every day.

but i loved you once,

so i want to die day after day.

# A Feel

here i am,  watching the sunset.
i wonder,
how do you look at the sunset and not see a punctured poetry?
this emptiness is killing me.
this feeling of agony is burning me up,
as if i am a wildfire.
but how do i show you this feeling?
it brings grief,  whenever i see,
someone else's heart in your arms,
like it's yours and keeping it like a gem with you as it's the only precious gem you are left with.
i think you are lost and i don't want to search you.
that's it.
i surrender.

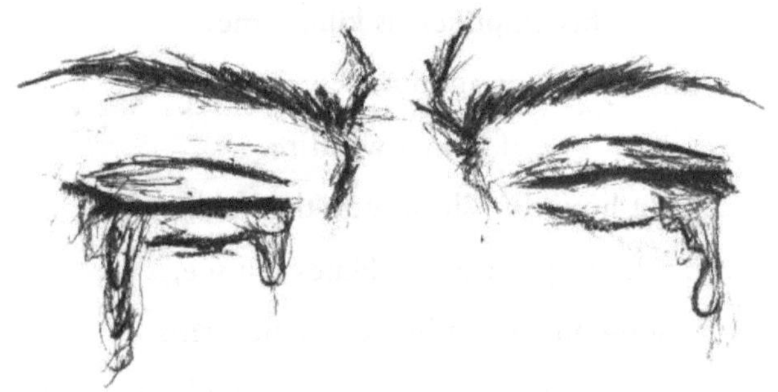

*two hearts, two souls, couldn't become one.*

# You – A Rash

once,
when i told you
i can write a book on you,
you laughed so hard,
that it made me cry.
then,
i told myself,
that you'll never make it into the pages of this book,
and see,
one whole section contains you.

# Soil

i wish i could hold you more tightly,
my grip just answered me back.
i am sorry.
you were like that soil,
which was hollow within deep.
and cannot afford to grow fruits and flowers on your stem.
i was trying hard,
to make you strong with pesticides on your roots,
unlike those who change the plant.

- why did i even tried?

# My story

i wonder, if you remember me?
i was craving for your love like a clock hand.
again and again,
on the same numbers.
the sun had already set on our love.
though,
with consistency and without composure,
i anticipate.
anticipate on our rising sun
(an image of our love, a feeling between you and me)
i was wrong.
the hazy and blurry images don' t actually work in this generation of clarity.
regardless,
when you heard my 13 year old love story, as a friend
i was so fragile and deprived of love and empathy.
that was the first time our vibes crossed and i actually thought about you.
that 13 year old me,
renounced hope on love.
but you,
you gave it a meaning again.

i again believed on cinderella and on puppy love.

i was so satisfied. thank you.

though,

i was lost trying to find you.

for you,

i prayed on my knees,

i begged for forgiveness

and left you for your contentment.

do you know why?

because i love you.

you are the reason behind the good marks in my love test,

you are the reason i have begun to believe in the sky for the answers.

but, i wish you could hear me.

sometimes my heart pangs that i cannot phrase my love in a way that you can understand.

# All Of Me

right at this moment,
your love doesn't fulfill me
but breaks me instead,
into billions of new pieces i haven't discovered yet.
my intoxic mind spells a word,
and remembers the sins done by the soul.
no doubt, i am shrinking
deep deep inside my wounds
i'm sinking.
my scars haunt me
as when i see the dead me inside the mirror.
dark dark and depressed answers found me
in the crowd of joy and contentment.
triggered was my soul and torn were the organs.
pouring rain can never get me back nor join my organs back,
into the world which is harmless and safe
though, it can harm me more and more.
i cry.
but my nostalgic tears are invisible
so, i scream,
but the world is deafen.

so i write,

but no one ever reads me.

but when i die,

each one wants me to be seen, to be heard

and

to read me.

including you.

out of curiosities,

each one will try to find me

inside the incomplete lyrics of a song

inside the torn pages of the books

or maybe

introspection.

but i,

i will be willingly transforming myself into the cosmo

and waving my way to solace.

# Forget Me

forget me,
forget my favorite books,
which we read half apart.
forget the page on which we left.
forget my hair bands,
which were of your favorite colors.
forget my nail paints,
which only painted love and art of passion and integrity.
forget my breaths,
which were heavy when you touched me.
forget my phone covers,
which said "love is love and no one can take its place".

forget my wallpapers,
which gave a glimpse of your heart from your pictures.
forget my films, reels and polaroids,
which showed your birthdays and only us.
forget my pillows, chargers and and key chains,
which had a smell of you.
forget
because i shared everything with you.
just forget,
but mind, i won't forget.

*the best in me is that there's nothing like you.*

## *What are you?*

you are so partial to my essence,
only fond of pretty faces.

# Guilty

dear lover, 12/02/2020

hurting wasn't my passion and still it isn't. but please forgive me, if possible. my mistakes have wounded you so deeply that i can see the blood forth on your skin and that bleeding eyes can now hurt me more intensely but wait, did you ever asked, why?

i wish you could, as if you thought we are fulfilled and contented. but no, we weren't.

i once thought we would end up sitting together and fighting for which bedside to take and quarrel on "wine or beer" like a perfect couple who lived next to us and never weeped out of breakups. but i know, i'm a poet and i imagined all of this while whining about how my mistakes are hurting like fresh and uncured wounds and thinking if they'll ever change into painfree scars?

- yours

- but not yours

# I Feel Like...

that's how i feel sometimes,
like i am frozen
or trapped
in somewhere
where my tears can't tickle my cheeks.

# Love A Spam

love is a fake story
impractical and extreme theory.
it refills all emotions while sleeping.
it is spam.
unsolicited.
but a question,
isn't it romanticizing all sorts of phases?
isn't this the beauty of romance?
i haven't answered any of them,
as it seeks love
to answer in detail.
and i don't fall for the fake stories
for the real ones
i rise.
- fallen for someone instead of rising with someone.

# I Am Tired

i'm giving up. i am tired.

tired of hoping things would work out better for me and my environment. unfortunately, it is never gonna happen. i'm extremely tired of seeking permissions for going to the doctor and taking risks to meet my best friend. i'm tired of crying and consoling myself from the quotes that say "you are absolutely capable of creating the life you can't stop thinking about. stop living in your head, it' s time to make your dreams happen. "

well, it's not. i know, i'm gonna be like my mother, strong from inside out, but an unindependent person. you know, it's always parents who make their child's life more worth surviving than living. i'm tired of hearing my friends saying "don't give up. " i'm tired, i can't now, i want to give up.

i am tired, tired of feeling pity on myself and crying on me. i'm tired of being unsettled and dark and blaming my mother for all of this.

i am fucking tired of writing my tiredness and tears and asking about why can't wrong be wrong and right be right? tired of hoping to make something new and tired of enjoying my own company. i am tired of being delayed in the place of urgency, tired to put my value behind the bushes, where no one can ever find it, tired of being a responsible person in the family, tired of frying myself in the pan of anger filled with my own oil of agony. i'm really really tired. i was trying very hard to get a normal life, but i have realized that it's not about how you feel, it's about how your environment feels. i thought i was growing and blooming day by day but what i'm actually doing is killing my road to an independent life.

i promise to be more quiet to show my liability because i am tired of speaking on freedom, tired of asking to fulfill my wishes as time has changed and you need to be self made. i am tired of planning things to make everyone feel like i am there for them, tired of feeling alone when in need of a hand.

i'm tired. please let me die, i wanna give up.

they cannot uplift their old thinking and i cannot live with their under lifted thoughts.

i gave him the moon and stars

but all he wants is

*space.*

*- orion carloto*

# Death

# Death

i am not emily dickinson
but i am me
who is waiting to see you every night
coming slowly towards my soul and body
and leisurely asking me for a dance
in the ball of dead bodies,
where living must be we two.
steadily making love and suddenly destroying some beautiful smiles.
but i love how you come,
silently,
peacefully,
asking life out.
immortality is not what i yearn for,
but death you are handsome.
i doubt, we share a picture perfect in my eyes,
but whenever we meet, you give me endless memories .
i know you love me, like a poet loves poetry.
do you realise, that when you call for me,
i skip some of my heartbeats.
i love how you whisper my name in my ears
and

slightly touch my neck with your breath.
i see myself for 20 times in the mirror when you call me for
a date
and
when you hold my red gown while perching on a horse
wagon, i see that love,
falling like tears from your beloved eyes.
i keep writing to you,
keeping my pleasures and pain behind the books which say –
"death is horrific and scary."
i want to know you more,
why? why do you pretend to be harmful?
you are so rich and filthy of lives.
prince or pauper
god or angel
once has to come to you.
even in my dreams when i find you,
hiding like a five year old, behind the bushes
to make me come to you,
i ask you to come for me.
turn my sleep into a deathful sleep,
take me away,
through my poetry, dreams and an eternal death.

# If I Die Tonight...

if i die tonight,
bury me, do not burn me,
put me back into the land.
put my favourite plumerias near me,
and some on my bed too.
spray a little, but one of my favourite
perfume in the air,
where my dead particles are visible
and
can get mixed with.
open my diaries and share everything with the world,
read all my poems which were never supposed to be out.
from my first draft to my last words,
read everything out loud.
but wait,
please do not mourn for me,
be happy that i could scout for death and track
about what's beyond it.

# Dear Death,

to whom
you kill human kinds.
i would say,
they don't deserve to be divine.
i have observed you
in most people.
coming and not leaving, is all your nature.
you stay with us, through tough and thins.
you don't kill people, instead you liberate them,
their souls and their bodies,
to sleep without interruption.
you take a walk through eternity.
they might fear you, but i really adore you.
you are an illusion of sleep and rest,
so aren't you giving us pleasures?
how can anyone frighten from you?
donne said,
"no man dies"
they get featured in an eternal life.
i think i believe that.

# Death's Greatest Mistake

when i seek life,
i see death.
and when i seek death,
i see death.
it makes me believe,
that i am no one's own.
nobody wants me,
as like, i am the death.
behind tears and sorrows,
i have funded my integrity
which is beyond everything and anyworld.
but death, you made a mistake.
you ate my ribs,
my lungs,
my intestines,
my skin,
my pancreas,
and all my fucking organs,
but you forgot to eat my heart.

hey, don't be afraid, i know how much you love me and live inside of me. there is only you and you and i couldn't resist thinking about you. you left my heart aching to beat for you and when it sighs, it actually aches for you. i'll make you realise that you have caused yourself a mistake. i want you to know that i want to cover every mistake of yours as it belongs to me. when the world writes about you, i want them to remember me, like the dead poets society.

- me to death

# Letter To The Dead Poet

dear dead poet,

i think you might learn something about me as i'm *someone who is more like you. but my words and your* words don' t match, but thoughts are carbon copied. i want you to know me like people know you. i know, i am a thief, stealing your naive but artful notions every now and then, but that's how i grow, like a bougainvillea which differs from you in the color but comes from the changeless breed. you have little sayings on bird, door, sleep, mirror, home, heart, mind, ears, pain, feelings, see, music, love, death, scars, faith, hope, events, grief, possibilities, funerals, garden, jewel, world, madness, a loaded gun, sisters, souls, success, surgeons, truth, pleasure, society, loneliness, slant of light, wild nights, history, conclusions, letters, legacies, riches, poverty and *i am nobody* in the context.

"i am nobody! who are you?

are you nobody too?

then there's a pair of us!

don't tell! they'd advertise – you know.

how dreary – to be – somebody!

how public – like a frog –

to tell one's name – the livelong june –

to an admirable bog! "

- emily dickinson

"if i read a book and it makes my whole body so cold, no fire can warm me up. i know that is poetry. if i feel physically as if the top of my head were taken off, i know that is poetry. these are the only ways i know it. is there any other way?"

- quote by - EMILY DICKINSON

writing to the most intense and romantic poet of the new england, i hope to meet you soon in my afterlife but until then, anticipating your reply on this letter will be my most fantasized wish to live on and to avoid my reality and work in the sense of imagination.

- me to emily dickinson

as by the dead we love to sit,

as by the dead we mourn.

# Corpses Are The Sexiest

i find solace and death
are two different things.
one comes momentarily
and
the other for eternity.
but i find,
both lay corpses and caskets of and for a humankind.
and that is very much to offer in the notion of one's thoughts
about allay and death,
of course.
that made me believe that aren't corpses have so much to offer?
if one can read them, with the idea of observation, can know that how beautifully they lay
without any crimps on the forehead
and sleep with a gentle reminder,
that there will be no interruptions nor there will be solace.
ones who wailed on them will realize
that one dies on land
and get solace in the arms of a coffin.
and laid corpses becomes the happiest out of all the pallbearers.

# Myths

i have heard myths
and gods are all they talk about when they say myths.
no devils and no demons,
no evils and no ghosts.
i live in a small town, where gardner narrates folk tales
and mother love fairies.
i once asked them,
how is a person deceased?
and why?
mother said,
" even god wants to be with good people and turn into fairies when they die. "
and the gardener said,
"death is better than life, better than the pain a living leads to.
death is beauty of sleep which one can only recognize,
when he is fast asleep for a very very long time. "

# A Reason To Die

if people can't die,
for what they believe in,
then is there any reason for death?
as a death rattle
one summons for inhumation
and offer lavenders and roses
to set the seal on their soul
for a walk in silhouette and plateful of stodge.
if it be the jinns of arabian,
or the father of all gods and humans, the zeus,
the lore makes it worth living today,
and will be tomorrow too.
being legendary heroes of a particular man,
these gods are versatile,
and with them,
death formally and informally conjoin.

# A Shadow

i am running far away,
with worries on my shoulders and fear in my head.
running to escape from the shadow,
who keeps supporting me,
when i'm alone.
the fact of my reality,
is that i am running from my own shadow.
frightening as if it will kill my death.
(for the reader who doesn't know i love death)
though i know,
how fiercely it says that it will live with me and dive with me
and will live until i breathe.
so now,
i'm inviting it to dance
letting it sway along with me and with romantic beats of time.
i ask it,
to sync footsteps as we twirl and laugh and love,
while perching for death together.

# Before

before my eyes are shut

i wanna see the whole sky, look beyond the clouds, stare at starry nights with constellations.

before my legs are burned,

i wanna run and escape from this crowd, breathe in an open world.

before my hands are chopped,

i wanna write thousands and millions of poems, which can make people feel more lonely and dead inside.

before my mouth is shut,

i wanna scream so loud that everyone can hear my wounds and see my pain from my noise.

before i die,

i wanna live like a free bee and sing like a blooming flower, dance on the beats of stardust

and wanna create magic,

a magic, with smell of fragility in it.

i wish i could see how death smelled.

# Death Come To Me

why are you taking so long to come to me?
when will you come for me,
to take me away from this place.
most people will be glad if you never came, but not me.
i always wanna see you
coming slowly and slowly taking all my breaths away.
look, you'll never regret taking me with you,
i'll never bother you and your chores.
i know, no one wants to see you,
no one wants to discuss you either and i feel genuine apologies for that.
not because you are no one's favorite or you take people away with you,
i wanna go with you
to see what's beyond you
why is there so much silence and darkness which symbolizes you,
why are people so afraid of you
i want to know
who you really are?

# An Unknown Tree

to have my sensuality i must have that courage to prove it too, worth having a flesh of my skin and emotions of my heart. deep down there, under the terra firma, i grow my roots to build my stem and step towards becoming a tree. now this tree has freckles on his face and shoulders, contains aromatic hydrocarbon and citrus to breathe in the flavour of dry wood notes and is fragile but looks strong. it has radiant skills, people love it, saves it from breaking it too, but watering isn't their call!

no filtering and no making of wines to help it to cognize childhood under it's shades and beliefs in lovers existence.

it wants to die instead. break it, supplant it from the given roots, extricate it's each stem from it's body, deplume it's leaves as if it is the season of fall and it's helping l'amant to romanticize and to put themselves into a soul of single life and when at last it will die, pluck it's fruits and share it with the world to know it's flair and enhance it's worth after death.

recall it's memories with you, hang polaroids with the strings made up of it, use a frame made up of paper which has a hint of it, living inside and looking onto them and you, hang them in your room, close to your bed and when it will remind you of the shades it gave, read and listen it's fruits.

absolutely, again and again and again.

liberate it. it dies for it.

*- i wish i could replace it with me*

# Stranger In My Head

i felt a stranger in my head.
i felt him.
he says, he is nobody.
but he is more like a snake to me.
crisp, blue eyes,
which makes me lost.
smooth and natural skin,
as i touch him i feel ranunculus kept on his skin.
his ears,
listen to all that i can't utter.
venomous and poisonous as hell,
he contains the power to kill me.
he slithers into me, wraps me and squeezes me,
until i can't breathe.
he is immense and enormous
like a giant wave.
so, so, powerful,
that i can't handle him for too long.
he bites,
like a wasp.
just a sting and the toxin extinguishes the fire of life.
and still,
he says, he is nobody.

# Afterdeath

people
after i die,
do not mourn,
reminisce.
make me feel sad,
that i'll leave everything behind and face my own truth, my reality.
do not wear dark clothes
not because they'll symbolize grief or sorrow,
but because i don't discriminate against colors
do not put roses on my grave,
not because they'll symbolize love and affection,
but because i don't like roses.
after death,
make me a sign of peace,
which can resolve warships and noises.
not because i want to be remembered like this,
but because all i want for the world is peace.

# I Know!

i know,
whom to give my wounds to aid!
i know,
how brutus killed caesar!
i know,
why do scars last longer than a man!
i know,
where people hide their emotions for the sake of love!
i know,
they don't hide,
they just wait to die.

**apparently, death is dark, i think death is the lightest**

# I Am In The Tomb

i am in the tomb,
buried deep into cement and marbles.
people come and go, like stars
glory and gone.
they don't even stay as long as the sun.
but like stars, varied and large.

i'm in the tomb,
buried deep into cement and marbles.
my tomb contains art
traditional as cast.
i see it daily with my closed eyes and unreminded scars.
i get no air to breathe and food to eat
but i still feel like i have more to sleep.

i am in the tomb
buried it deep into cement and marbles.
they make confessions near me,
mourn to remember and memories to capture
but all i gotta do is,
lay like a dead man and reckon with the trapper.

i'm in the tomb

buried deep into cement and marbles.

i store deep dark secrets,

where lover kissed someone else on the shore and father killed his own son,

like a brother who knew he would do drugs and a sister who tries nothing but to slug.

dares like a devil,

but shares like an angel.

finding my solace from this dried skull.

i am in the tomb,

buried deep into cement and dark marbles,

but it feels like i am all seen.

# Dead Poets Society

i wish
i could create art
like the dead poets created.
exactly what i felt and fantasized.
plentiful of musings running inside my mind,
racing on, which word will win.
this maddening hunger strikes every now and then.
i can write
through mental breakdowns and until suffocation,
and until i start choking.
the words lingering after and after,
i couldn't stop but to puke them on the paper.
i write and i run,
not out of words but of time.
i kicked them out, beat them and stretch to figure,
why is it just a free verse?
rhyming, metaphors and similes
aren't destructive to focus,
but when i wail, cry and scream my words out
i can only hear them back
from the diaries which reflected
moroseness and that of the powerful play

which goes on and in which i may contribute a verse.

so, if it is a sonnet or an acrostic,

my diaries will be full of blood,

as i'll bleed poetry,

and living long will be the

*dead poets society.*

# Ladder of years

from the days, i was a monster, till the day i'm calling someone a monster, i have grown up.

i wish being quiet and kind was easy like being a rageous monster. but it's not, unfortunately.

in this passion and rage, anger and brazenness, i have been hurt and have hurt people, feelings, ashes and my earphones, a lot!

but again, unfortunately, people complain and ashes scare me.

i have injured my own heart in a way that it can bleed and sacrifice its mutuality to have emotions and love out of all the details and ways. i know, i cannot love, selflessly selfish i am,

but i am a happy monster who is proudly surviving these years, months, days, hours, minutes and every second of this cloudless infinite sky.

the first 100 days, were like golden days of me being a fucking little kind and more of an arrogant monster. i was tough, painful, tired and exhausted from the severe damage to my heart.

the next 100 days were like pure blood red days, which called off the knives on my doors of heart and dealt with

some bloody paranormal maniacs of my broken brain/ which
shows no concern out of no where.

the next to next 100 hundred days were like me being a

perfect monster, i had the monster' s eye, knowing there is
no such thing called a friend, escaping from love and care,
vigorously saving my time for the bitter and antipathetic
truth of life.

i knew another coming sixty five days would probably
please me to go into my dark but safe side.

so i lived.

came 65 days...

long but smaller than affection,

deep but shallower than greetings,

narrow but wider than love.

i haven't stopped living but i have crossed living that
monstrous stage of my infinite cloudless sky.

i came up with an another year,

an eye of a saint,

fought against my previous year's demons.

but i knew, i wasn't toxic,

good or evil,

i cannot attract.

i was/am

dumb

a cute moron.

but i am a proud me as well.

because after surviving black and intoxicated days of my life,

i got my sweet little whites.

i am strong and there is no such thing that i cannot really do,
better decision to choose what to do and what not to will always be mine and difficult as well.

it's not about a man and a woman,

it's all about what you make – cloudless sky or a sky full of clouds.

it's about what you choose – to drink coffee or to not to prefer beverages at all,

it's all of your consent.

# If I Should Die And You Should Live...

if i should die
and you should live,
and time should gurgle on
and morn should beam
and noon should burn
and evening should kiss
for shops should stare
and talk should hills
and forest should laugh
and dance should leaves
and bees should sing
if bird should build
and sun should sit
and bugs should fly
and bloom should daisies
and moon should eclipse
and souls should love
meanwhile – apocalypse.

*do you sell time? i don't bother if you do, because all i am saving is for death.*

# Acknowledgements

First and foremost, I would love to thank my dada, for investing in me and taking a big risk. Massive thankyou to my chachu, for being there in every single brutal step of all of me's journey. Thanks to ananya and amma for keeping me motivated during all worst times, it wouldn't be possible without these strong and gentle ladies.

Thanks to my publisher, bluerose for bringing this soul to life, my second baby, my all of me.

A big thankyou to my illustrator, Ms. Bhavya sharma, my classmate and an enhanced artist.

Lastly,

My many thanks to my readers for reading me and giving me a chance to make up your mind by my words. Thankyou for trusting me enough to have even made it to this page.

Never thought that I would write books when I was 7 year old, but always believed that god is there with me, by my side.

Thankyou god.

# About The Author

Nandini Joshi is an author and a poet, born in Kolkata, India and raised in small town of Rajasthan. Her first book was on philosophical aspects of life and on 11 important life lessons one should adapt. The book is named as "My 11 life percepts" which is available on amazon, flipkart and kindle.

Pulled up inspiration from some of the most intense and romantic poets of the bygone era - Emily Dickinson, John Donne, John Keats, Amrita Pritam, Gulzar and many more, She got herself engaged in poetry and gave birth to her second book – all of me.

Nandini enjoys collecting mugs and perfumes and grooves on folk, punjabi, hollywood and bollywood songs which makes her more of her.

Join her on instagram and facebook - @___firstborn___

9 789354 728877

Printed by Libri Plureos GmbH in Hamburg, Germany